Invitation to Faith

John Macquarrie

Invitation to Faith

SCM PRESS LTD

ISBN 0 334 02587 7

Originally delivered as lectures during Lent 1994 by invitation of the Vicar of St Andrew's, Old Headington, Oxford, Fr Michael Brewin, and the Parochial Church Council.

First published 1994
under the title *Starting from Scratch*
by Harold Copeman, Oxford

Second edition published 1995
by SCM Press Ltd
26–30 Tottenham Road, London N1 4BZ

Phototypeset by Intype, London
and printed in Great Britain by
Mackays of Chatham, Kent

Contents

Foreword

by the Right Reverend John V. Taylor, formerly Bishop of Winchester

As a communicator Professor Macquarrie has the gift of rapid acceleration, a rare skill among theologians: within a few sentences he can get the reader's mind racing. For example, he opens the first of these chapters, originally lectures, by observing that human beings, ever since their earliest appearance on this planet, seem to have been creatures that worshipped; yet a moment later he has one wondering whether it is in fact necessary to have any belief at all.

There is a wide spectrum of disbelief today in the former heartlands of Christianity, and many Muslims in fact hold Christianity itself responsible for this. At one extreme of the spectrum lies religiosity without a god, where worship survives as a technique for the cultivation of self-awareness. Next to that comes intellectual disbelief based upon lack of evidence; then moral disbelief which finds the propositions and, even more, the conduct of religious bodies objectionable. At the other end is the broad band of what can better be described as non-belief – those innumerable men and women who have been too absorbed in their mundane survival to find time for those questions of ultimate meaning to which the only answer is a leap of faith. Such were the Welsh hill-farmers of whom R. S. Thomas wrote his early poems and whom he calls 'your prototype – an impregnable fortress'. Such, too, are the majority of our wholly secularized consumers in this stressful and competitive society of ours.

Are they actually the poorer for their lack of religious belief? Or has the ancestral sense of God become as unnecessary as such physical endowments as wisdom teeth or the appendix? Morality does not depend upon religion; yet a religious definition of what it means to be human certainly adds some important criteria by which to judge what is right or wrong. Those who believe that in the last resort they can be 'compared with the beasts that perish' may feel more free to apply that valuation when they legislate for the status of human embryos or defectives. Furthermore, religion is a powerful source of cultural cohesion and, although this has often worked for intolerance, no one can claim that the present atomization of society is making people happier or more free. Or again there is sound evidence that people who never ask or answer the question about the meaning of their existence are deprived of what is probably the greatest resource for mental health. It has been well said that 'they who have a *why* to live can bear with almost any *how*'.

Yet the only valid reason for seeking to change disbelief or non-belief is not that it is socially or psychologically advantageous, but that it is the truth, and what inhibits Christians from commending their personal faith naturally to all and sundry is neither lack of training nor even embarrassment so much as lack of conviction.

That is the point at which these four chapters, with the questions and answers that follow each of them, should make their most powerful impact. *Invitation to Faith*, as its title suggests, is certainly readable and understandable enough to appeal to anyone who has either been put off religion or never been drawn towards it. Such a one can hardly fail to be disarmed by Macquarrie's undogmatic honesty and intrigued by his skilful explanations. Yet even greater, perhaps, will be the book's value in helping tongue-tied believers to realize that they need not be ashamed to admit the many questions to which they have to answer 'I don't know' or 'I can't explain' because there is enough in their faith that is so certain and exhilarating that they can no longer keep it to themselves.

I

Why Believe?

No one can say with certainty how many thousands or perhaps even hundreds of thousands of years human beings
have been living on this planet. But one thing that can be
said is that however far back research has been able to go,
there are signs that these ancestors of ours all cherished some
religious faith. Human beings have been worshipping beings.
They have believed that there is a reality beyond the human,
and that belief has of course been enormously influential in
shaping human history. Not only individuals, but great cultures have owed a vast debt to their religious beliefs and
have tried to embody these beliefs in the practical ordering
of their lives.

But this state of affairs, which has lasted for so long, has
changed quite dramatically. The change began here in the
western world, and has gone much further here than anywhere else, though it is now also affecting other cultures.
That change began around the middle of the eighteenth
century in the great intellectual revolution which we call the
Enlightenment. What took place could be described as a kind
of 'coming of age' of the human race. Up to that time, people
had recognized certain authorities that had been since the
distant past, such as the church and the Bible in matters of
faith and morality, the monarchy in politics, ancient writers
such as Aristotle in matters of philosophy and science. But
now these ancient authorities were all being put in question.
People wanted to know if there were any good reasons for
accepting these authorities. After all, life had not been all
that wonderful under the old regimes. Poverty and hard

labour had been the lot of most people, while disease, constant wars and other forms of violence meant that life was
precarious for everybody. Would not the human race do
better for itself if it discarded the influence of the past and if
people began to think for themselves and act for themselves,
regardless of what the Bible or Aristotle or any other revered
authority might have taught? Was there not already an
example of the possibilities of new and liberating thought in
the rising sciences of that time? Copernicus, for instance,
had already put forward his theory that the earth goes round
the sun, rather than the sun's going round the earth: and
although this theory seemed to challenge the creation story
in Genesis, people soon saw that it makes much more sense,
for it gives a more intelligible picture of the solar system.
This was only the beginning of a long series of disputes
between scientists and conservative believers, creating a ten-
sion in the public mind that has lasted to the present day.

As a result, at the end of the twentieth century, we in the
West are living in a culture in which religious belief has been
largely discarded. For the first time in the history of the
human race, there exists a godless culture, a people with no
religious belief.

Of course, that is not entirely the case. There are many
people who still have a faith and practise a religion, while
among those who say they have no religion there have sprung
up new cults and there has even been a revival of such
superstitions as astrology. Others have adopted fundamentalism, a dogmatic uncritical return to supposedly traditional
beliefs. But even so, the past two hundred and fifty years
have been marked by a steady decline of religion in the West
and a corresponding growth of secularism. So before we
begin talking about Christian faith and expounding its content, we have to ask the preliminary question, 'Why bother
with faith at all?' Today a great many people seem to get
along with no religious belief. So we find ourselves asking
the question, 'Why believe?'

A first step toward answering that question is just to notice that as human beings, we cannot help asking questions. We have minds that think and we have decisions to make, and as soon as we come to the age of responsibility, we begin asking questions, and we go on asking questions as long as we live. Our questions do not arise just out of idle curiosity. They are questions that touch on our lives and what we are doing with our lives. I once heard an Oxford don, the late Austin Farrer, make a typically Oxonian remark: he said 'It seems terribly improbable that we should exist'. Has it ever struck you that it does seem very odd that you and I exist? Here we are, thrown into a world in which we have to live. We did not choose to exist, we did not create ourselves nor did anyone consult us as to whether we wanted to live. It has just happened to us that we have, so to speak, wakened up in a world and grown up in a world, where we become conscious that we have to make our lives with whatever resources we have and along with all the other people who have to make their lives in the same world.

So if we use our minds at all, we cannot help wondering what is going on. What is it all about? Is there any meaning to it? Paul Tillich suggested that even if many people nowadays are not afflicted with the sense of sin, they have a new problem; they are afflicted with the sense of meaninglessness. Life, for many people, seems to be just one thing after another with no coherent pattern and no goal in view. But if anyone asks, 'Does my life have any meaning or any value? Where have I come from? Where am I going?' such a person soon discovers that there are no certain answers to these questions. No one can prove beyond doubt either that there is a meaning and purpose to human life, or that there is no such meaning and purpose. Here believers and agnostics are in the same boat. The famous American philosopher, William James, ends his essay, 'The Will to Believe' (*Selected Papers on Philosophy*, Dent, 1917, p. 124), with a quotation from an English Victorian writer, which gives eloquent expression to the fact that we do not know with the certainty we would like why we are living at all: 'What do you think of yourself?

What do you think of the world? These are questions with which we must all deal. They are riddles of the Sphinx, and yet, in one way or another, we must all deal with them. In our important transactions, we must take a leap. If we decide to leave the riddle unanswered, that is a choice. Whatever choice we make, we make it at our peril. If a man chooses to turn his back altogether upon God, no one can prevent him, no one can show beyond reasonable doubt that he is mistaken. We stand on a mountain pass, in the midst of whirling snow and blinding mist, through which we get glimpses now and then of paths which may be deceptive. If we stand still, we shall be frozen to death. If we take the wrong road, we shall be dashed to pieces. We can only act for the best and hope for the best.'

Some points in this quotation deserve to be pondered carefully. Though we are told that we cannot know beyond the shadow of doubt which way to go, we are also told that we must deal with the questions. That is part of our finite human condition. We have to answer questions without always having a fully convincing proof of the answers that we give. This happens to be true of all the most important questions in our lives. It is true, for instance, in economics and politics, as well as religion. By our very deeds and decisions every day in our lives, we are giving answers to the questions of what we think of ourselves and what we think of the world. That is why we must venture on beliefs that go beyond what we certainly know. To return to our quotation, 'In our important transactions, we must take a leap.' Call it, if you like, the 'leap of faith' – the step which takes us beyond what we can know with certainty into a realm where we can be content only with belief or disbelief. Of course, we do not take such a step lightly. We do not believe just anything, though unfortunately men and women have often been persuaded to accept beliefs that have no basis, and they have suffered the consequences of their gullibility. So when we accept a belief, conscience demands that we should weigh it as carefully as we can, and this is especially the case with those serious beliefs affecting religion and morality. Such beliefs are more than just intellectual opinions – they are acts of faith which influence our actions and our whole way of life.

There are of course some people – perhaps they would call themselves positivists – who would say that they entertain no beliefs that go beyond those matters of fact for which definite empirical evidence can be obtained. They might tell us that it is enough for human beings to get on with their lives in this world and not bother about 'ultimate' questions concerning God and the 'meaning' of life and suchlike.

But if these 'ultimate' questions are not just intellectual opinions but have a practical bearing on how we live, I doubt if we can opt out of them. People who disclaim having any profound beliefs about themselves or about the significance or insignificance of human existence in the world perhaps do have such beliefs deep down in themselves, though they have never thought them out. The very actions they perform and the values they seek to realize testify to what these unconscious beliefs are. Bertrand Russell, for instance, was one of the most notable atheists of his generation, but his profound commitment to the cause of peace and some of the things which he wrote about peace are evidence of a deep reverence on his part for the moral demand that is made on every human being. Karl Rahner has made much of the idea of the 'anonymous Christian', the person who, while unwilling or unable to affirm Christian beliefs, is nevertheless committed to at least some fundamental Christian values. I do not myself care much for the expression, 'anonymous Christian', for I think that it does not sufficiently respect the person's intellectual wrestling with, and eventual rejection of, Christian belief: but there is some validity in the idea that where there is a practical obedience to Christian ideals, there is also some implicit acceptance of the beliefs which underlie these ideals. On the other hand, a person who subscribed in the most minute detail to orthodox Christian belief in, let us say, the doctrine of the triune God, but whose actual life was not in conformity with the belief, would have to be adjudged hypocritical.

There are, I think, two basic questions about which everyone has to come to some decision, especially in the crises of life. Both questions were mentioned in the passage which I quoted earlier. The first was, 'What do I think of myself?' or, more briefly, 'Who or what am *I*?' Almost every day we are called on to give various partial answers to this question, depending on the circumstances of the question. If I were on a trip abroad, I might say, 'I am a British subject'; In a social gathering, I might say, 'I am a priest of the Anglican communion'. In other contexts, I might say that I am a graduate of Oxford or a husband and father or whatever would be appropriate. Yet so many of these descriptions are superficial or even cover-ups. They relate to the various functions and roles that we engage in. We could go on adding such descriptions, but possibly only in a real crisis do we come to the ultimate question – who is it who appears in all these roles? Suppose they were all stripped away, who or what, if anything, would be left?

In the years after World War II there was published in Germany a book about the human condition as it was seen at that time. One section of it was called 'the Man from the Hut'. It introduced us to a man who must have been one of multitudes at that time, and who are still to be found today. He had been stripped of virtually everything, with only his basic humanity left. The man was a refugee from eastern Europe, now living in an overcrowded hut in what had once been a military camp. Once he had had a wife and two children, as well as numerous friends, once he had had a home and a well-stocked farm, once he had had the comforts of life and what we call a respected place in society. But the invading armies had rolled across his part of the world, he had lost farm and family and friends alike, and now he is thrown back on himself. A crisis indeed! For the first time in his life, the question 'Who are you?' is thrust upon him in a radical way. As the man puts it, 'Well, tell me, who am I, then, and what am I living for, and what is the sense of it all?' This is an extreme case, and I suppose none of us would expect ever to be in a parallel situation, though we cannot be too sure, for such things are still happening even in Europe today. But it is unlikely that we shall escape some situation that will make us deeply question what our lives are all about. We can never fully know the answer to the question, but, as I have already said, we cannot help answering it to the best of our powers. The kind of answer that we give can be tested to some extent by the degree to which it enables us to live more effectively and to stand up to the trials that have provoked the crisis.

The Christian answer to the question about the identity of each one of us has two parts to it. It tells us that we are finite, imperfect, yes, even sinful creatures. We are not God, and even handling our own lives is something that we cannot do on our own. We have to look beyond ourselves to a wisdom that is divine rather than human, for a grace that can strengthen us in our weakness. And the testimony of generations of Christians has been that when men and women do that, they are indeed helped and strengthened.

On the other hand, the experiment of living without God as people have been doing increasingly in the past two hundred years has led to the kind of situation in which the man in the hut (and remember he is only one who has happened to be noticed among a vast multitude) has been brought to the very margin of existence.

These remarks do not prove anything about the relative advantages of the Christian and the secular ways of life. Both have their ambiguities. There were plenty of evils in the old pre-Enlightenment days when Christianity had things all its own way and missed its chances. There are also good things in the secular culture, for instance, the much improved health of peoples all over the world. But what seems to be beyond doubt is that there has been no advance whatever in justice, morality and love. If Christianity holds out to us these gifts, then it has more claim on our belief than any of its rivals.

There is another side to the Christian answer to the question about human identity, a more affirmative side. It appeals not just to our weakness and our need of God's help, it appeals also to our strength and to the great possibilities that lie dormant in every human being. For the human being, according to biblical teaching, was created in the image of God and has within him or her that image, to act as a guide or a magnet to draw each one nearer in likeness to God. Our prayers to God and our worship of God are the means by which this precious gift within is strengthened and developed. Again, no one can produce any proof of the spiritual nature of man, just as no one can disprove it. But once more, when we set out on that path, we find that it does in a practical way enrich our lives and lift them to new levels.

There were two questions that confronted us. The first of them was 'What do you think of yourself?' and I have just been trying to answer that. The second question was 'What do you think of the world?', and it is to that question we must now turn.

Again, I think we have to acknowledge that what we see is ambiguous, and no proof is possible either way. The world of nature is full of beauty, and even of what looks like wisdom of an infinitely high order. But over against that we have to set the enormous amount of waste and destruction. Believers and unbelievers have argued over such questions for a very long time, and neither side has made out its case decisively and once for all. There are always new arguments and fresh evidences to be taken into account. The argument between faith and atheism, so far as it depends on an appeal to nature, has ended in stalemate.

But Christianity has never rested its case on appeals to natural theology, as it is called. Rather, the risk of faith has been taken on the ground of certain outstanding events that lit up a whole series of other events, and, as Christians believe, are nothing less than revelation. For the Israelites more than three thousand years ago there began a series of events in their history that clinched the matter for them. I mean, their deliverance from Egypt, their crossing of the Red Sea, their receiving the law through Moses, their becoming a nation in the wilderness, their pilgrimage to the promised land. This was for them the clue or paradigm that gave a meaning to everything in this world, and that led to their faith in God, the unseen power who calls the oppressed out of slavery, sets them free for a new life, places a law in their hearts, builds them up into a community that has order, dignity and hope. That is the faith that has kept Israel going through all the disasters from the sieges of Jerusalem many centuries ago down to the Holocaust in our own century.

We Christians have a different story as our paradigm. We believe that with all its ambiguities, this world is God's world, because of Jesus Christ, who, as John's Gospel tells us, is like a light shining in the darkness, and the darkness does not overcome it. His life, his teaching, his death, his resurrection, above all, his unconquerable love, are so over-whelmingly impressive that we confess that in him we have seen the glory of the Father, full of grace and truth. In him, something new entered the world, a life so compelling in its love and outreach to all that we accept him as the revelation of the deepest reality. It is in him that we learn what human life is about and what this world is about.

This is no arbitrary belief, nor is it a wishful belief. It is a reasonable belief, and one which, if we accept it, presents the greatest moral and spiritual challenge to be found anywhere.

Why believe? We all need something or someone to believe in. Jesus Christ invites us to believe in him, and I do not think that those who do so will be disappointed.

Questions and Answers

Q. *This question is about the nature of science. It is not claimed that science has the answer to all our questions, but*

*it is advancing all the time. Also, the kind of answers that
scientists give have a universality about them. What is true
in one place is true in another. Does this common mind
among scientists contrast with disagreement among theologians and religious believers?*

A. There are, of course, various theologies and even various religions, and they speak with a variety of voices. Nevertheless, especially in recent times, there has been much
dialogue between representatives of different views. This has
been true among Christian theologians, for instance, in the
Anglican-Roman Catholic Conversations (ARCIC) and even
more strikingly in the dialogues between representatives of
different religions – dialogues between Christians and Jews,
or between Christians and Muslims. This is surely not very
different from what happens in the sciences, when two inves-
tigators come up with different theories and then a discussion
takes place to try to sort out the competing claims. In inter-
religious dialogue, what comes to light is common ground,
but also continuing difference. Such inter-religious dialogue
is still relatively new, but it is surely a great gain that in the
tightly-knit world of today, when our activities all react on
one another, dialogue has replaced the earlier Christian atti-
tude which often dismissed the non-Christian religions as
merely error.

Q. *If different religious groups, for example, Christians
and Jews, tell different stories, how does one discriminate
among these stories? Are some of the stories to be rejected?*

A. Stories embody beliefs, and theologians try to isolate
the beliefs underlying the various stories so that it is easier
to compare and evaluate them. Christians share with Jews
the creation stories of the Old Testament, but they also have
their own stories based on the New Testament, and at this
point the differences between Judaism and Christianity
emerge. If one thinks of the differences between Christ-

ianity and the religions of eastern Asia, then some of them
appear to be much greater. The Judaeo-Christian story of the
creation of the world by God implies that the world is good,
as indeed God himself said in the story (Genesis 1.31); but
in the religions of the further east the material world is
generally accounted to be evil. Is there any way of bridging
this gap?

Again, in Christianity and Judaism, God is understood as
a personal being. But in eastern religions, God or the Holy
reality is often taken to be impersonal. Again, this seems like
a gulf that cannot be crossed. Yet here too points of similarity
are to be found. What the Buddhists call 'compassion' is not
far from what the New Testament calls 'love'.

As I mentioned, we are still in only the early stages of
inter-religious dialogue. As it goes on, more common ground
will be discovered. But it is likely that some differences will
remain. But do we need to be too much worried about this,
if mutual respect also remains? People are, after all, different,
and differences, provided they do not become bitter and
divisive, are actually an enrichment of the human race. It is
generally recognized nowadays that a measure of pluralism
in a society is a strength rather than a weakness, provided
that pluralism does not become destructive.

Believing in God

In the nineteen-sixties there broke out in the Christian church a debate concerning the most fundamental of all Christian beliefs, namely, belief in God. The debate began in England in 1963 when Bishop John Robinson published his famous paperback, *Honest to God*. That book was not a very profound or original piece of theology, but it was far more influential and reached far more people than most theological writings do. Robinson had sparked off a debate that took even himself by surprise. He frankly questioned whether the traditional conceptions of God, those that are popularly held in our churches, are still viable in the twentieth century. These common ideas of God think of him as a kind of universal monarch, a 'Louis XIV of the heavens', as William James once expressed it. This God of popular belief was a somewhat terrifying figure, and many people seemed to think that his principal function was to punish sin. This was a picture of God derived more from the Old Testament than from the New. Bishop Robinson wanted us to rethink our understanding of God, and in particular to get closer to the New Testament where God is a God of love, not in any weak or sentimental sense, but a God of self-giving love, as we see it in Jesus Christ. Soon, however, the debate had gone far beyond what Robinson had visualized. Some Christian theologians, especially in the United States, were saying that Christianity must dispense with the idea of God altogether. They told us that there is no place for God in the modern world, and if there is still a place for Christianity, it must be a form of Christianity that does not include belief in God.

The 'death of God' movement, as it was called, did not get very far in America, but it did spread to England and still has a certain following here. You may think, of course that the whole idea of a Christianity without God is self-contradictory, and it probably is. But it reflects the mood of the age. To many people of our time, belief in God presents difficulties. We have to acknowledge that some of these difficulties have been due to the poor teaching of the church about God. There has been too much stress on the power and rule of God, and too little on his love, condescension and humility. So the church itself, through distorted teaching, has been partially responsible for the decline of belief in God. To think of God primarily in terms of power is to go back to the old pagan ideas of God, such as Jupiter at Rome, or Marduk in Babylon, divine figures that were modelled on the despotic emperors of these ancient states. Christianity, with its teaching that God had become incarnate in Jesus Christ, revolutionized the understanding of God. It did not deny God's power as the creator and disposer of all things, but it insisted that God is not only above us but among us, indwelling the world, even appearing in the form of a servant and sharing the suffering of his creatures. But that revolution in the understanding of God was so complete that even after two thousand years we have not properly comprehended it. If we did understand it better and teach it better, I think many of the barriers that keep people from believing in God would be overcome.

What then are these difficulties? We have to try to understand them; and even those of us who may think we firmly believe in God may sometimes feel the force of the difficulties, and experience doubt in our own hearts. The first point to recognize is that there are different forms of atheism. In this book I want to distinguish three kinds of atheism, each expressing a distinct kind of difficulty in believing. But I think that a truly Christian and balanced understanding of God can meet these difficulties.

The first kind of atheism to consider is what may be

called intellectual atheism. What place is there for God, as traditionally conceived, in a world which we now understand in terms of the natural sciences? Is not this scientifically conceived world a self-regulating, self-sufficient system, in which everything that happens is explicable in terms of other happenings within the same system? Do we need to suppose that there is another reality, namely, God, in addition to the world itself, or is the world the ultimate reality, without needing any further grounding? At the beginning of this century, many scientists and materialist philosophers would have said that the universe has been in existence since all eternity, and that we need not suppose there is any creator God. But more recently scientists have been telling us that there was indeed a beginning to the universe, what is usually called the 'big bang', a primaeval explosion of energy fifteen or twenty thousand million years ago, and all the galaxies and stars and planets and whatever is found among them, including ourselves, had their origins in that great flash of energy. Even to acknowledge a beginning is to have moved closer to the biblical idea of creation. But we must not move too fast. Can we or should we ask about a creator who is behind that big bang and who originated it? Does it make sense to imagine anything before that first originative event, or must we not say that time itself began in that moment? It might be difficult to think of a God who pre-existed outside and entirely separate from the world-process, but if we think in more definitely Christian terms of a God who from the very beginning is above but also indwelling the universe, giving to it its ordered character, then I think it becomes much more acceptable to acknowledge the place of God in the world as science understands it.

Indeed, I think it would be fair to say that science today is much more hospitable to the idea of God than it was two or three generations ago. In spite of all the advances of the sciences, the ultimate mystery remains mysterious; each new discovery opens up a fresh mystery. I believe that at the present moment, physics has led us in the direction of a religious interpretation of the world, while perhaps biology remains somewhat hostile. But the picture is still an ambiguous one, in which some evidences seem to point to God, others away from him. But belief or disbelief, as I said in Chapter 1, 'Why Believe?', does not rest on balancing up these evidences. It may be enough to say that as far as the intellectual difficulties which the scientific view of the world presents for belief in God are concerned, there has taken place what Professor Keith Ward has called a 'turn of the tide'. But this depends on also accepting (and again I use Professor Ward's words) 'that God is not an object apart from the universe, of which we can only detect faint traces – but the mind and heart of the universe itself. To believe in God is to believe that at the heart of all reality, all this very reality in which we exist, is spirit, consciousness, value, reason, and purpose' (in *Holding Fast to God*, SPCK, 1982 p.5). This way of conceiving God stresses his indwelling of the world, whereas the traditional language stressed rather his difference from and his 'transcendence' of the world.

But there are not only intellectual difficulties in the way of believing in God. Perhaps even more influential have been the emotional factors in atheism. We have seen in the first chapter that the Enlightenment could be understood as a kind of coming of age of the human race, a phase in its development when men and women took over responsibility for their own existence and ceased to depend on external powers. In modern times, human beings have claimed autonomy, and it must be acknowledged that, as they expanded their knowledge and control of nature, life became more secure and tolerable as education, medicine and economic well-being developed. Human beings were doing things for themselves, while God seemed to become increasingly redundant or unnecessary.

Some, indeed, began to think of God as not merely redundant but as a barrier to human progress. The enormously influential teaching of Karl Marx, for instance, claimed that belief in God and the worship of God caused man to revolve round a false sun, so neglecting his tasks in this present world. Friedrich Nietzsche went even further. Human beings must recognize that God is dead, and strike out for themselves. They must become what he called 'supermen', the new rulers of the universe, taking over from the dead God; and, in spite of the risks, Nietzsche believed that the coming super-race would bring into being a better world than had ever been known in the ages of faith.

It is clear that this emotional atheism, this passionate rebellion against God in the name of humanity itself, is directed against that sub-Christian or even pagan idea of God as the supreme monarch, exercising a tyrannous rule over the world. It is a strange irony that the notion of the 'death of God' which was understood by Nietzsche in an atheist sense was originally a Christian idea and symbolized the distinctively Christian thought of God as one who is not securely throned above the world but is rather one who indwells the world and suffers with the creatures. It was a Lutheran hymn-writer, Johannes Rist, who in 1641 wrote a hymn for Good Friday which included the line 'God himself lies dead'. This line was so startling, even shocking, to worshipping congregations that it was later changed to 'The Lord himself lies dead'. But the point of the hymn-writer remains. If God was in Christ, then in some sense God suffered in and with Christ. When we understand that, then we understand also that God is no distant tyrant against whom we should rebel but one who has identified himself with mankind and indeed with his whole creation.

We turn now to a third type of atheism, what I shall call moral atheism. What lies behind this atheism is neither an intellectual difficulty nor an emotive rebellion against an all-powerful ruler, but a wholesome moral protest against the injustices and the apparently pointless sufferings of the creatures. This is not so much an atheism as an anti-theism: that is to say, the person who holds such a view is not so much denying that God exists as denying that any being who created a world as bad as ours is worthy to be called God, or to be worshipped. This is perhaps the oldest form of the denial of God – we find hints of it in the Book of Job and in some of the Psalms. The American rabbi Richard Rubenstein in recent years declared that after the Holocaust he could no longer believe in a righteous God who was guiding his chosen people Israel, though he did not deny that there might be a God of some sort. The French writer Albert Camus is another example of a modern rebel against the traditional belief in God. He urged that we must not resign ourselves to the evil of this world – we must rebel against the creation and the creator, even if we know in advance that such a rebellion is doomed to failure. In what he thinks is a meaningless world, Camus claimed that at least there is meaning in the human protest against it. Yet, in strict logic, the protest must be just as absurd and meaningless as everything else, though it may have more tragedy and more pathos about it.

Perhaps the most powerful statement of a moral or protest atheism has come not from an actual philosopher but from a fictional character, Ivan, in Dostoyevsky's famous novel *The Brothers Karamazov*. Ivan was not an intellectual atheist, for he says 'I accept God'. But what Ivan cannot accept is the world which God is said to have created. He believed that there is no possibility of finding a convincing argument that the creator of this world could be righteous or just, or (still less) loving. The fact that children suffer, and suffer very severely, is for Ivan an unanswerable objection to the belief that there is a loving God. Even the most ingenious arguments that good may come out of suffering would never justify the ills that people of all generations have seen around them.

This is obviously a very subtle form of atheism or antitheism, and one that has a strong appeal to sensitive persons. Yet even Ivan's rejection of God has its dangers and temptations. There is a kind of titanic pride in a human being who, so to speak, takes on the universe and appoints himself champion of the human race against – against, we must say, he is not quite sure what. A God who is not really God? Ivan wishes no part in this wicked world. In his own words, he respectfully returns his ticket.

Yet how much of the evil that distresses him is due to human agency, perhaps even to those who have been loudest in their claim to be autonomous in ordering their own lives without regard to God? In contrast to Rabbi Rubenstein, another writer of Jewish background, Ulrich Simon, in his book *A Theology of Auschwitz* (Gollancz 1967) considers a situation very like the one which so deeply troubled Ivan Karamazov, but he came to a very different view. He gives us a moving glimpse of the children unwittingly entering the gas-chambers at Auschwitz, some of them clutching their dolls and teddy-bears, and he goes on to say 'The children of Auschwitz convict us of an undefinable darkness – the evil is of such dimensions that it discloses an unsuspected degree of guilt in the whole human race, and it is this knowledge of evil that cries out for an atonement which no man can work.'

We should notice also that there is a strange contradiction in what Ivan says. We have seen that he says 'I return my ticket', but he also says 'I want to live'. There is a temptation to exaggerate beyond what is justifiable the gloom and miseries of human life in this world. We all know that there are vast amounts of suffering in the world, and likewise vast amounts of human sin, but there are also innumerable moments of joy, hope and love. It is, of course, impossible and perhaps even rather silly to attempt any quantitative reckoning that might show that the good exceeds the evil or might one day exceed it, and we can understand how attempts to argue along such lines could only exasperate a sensitive person like Ivan. But the crucial point appears to me to be this – that the sufferers themselves and those who like Ivan sympathize with them, say they *want to live*. They want the experiment of human life to continue. They recognize that there are great potentialities here to realize. They may talk of returning the ticket, but only a few very sad people do that, and then as a last resort. Even those for whom we might think that life has nothing good to offer keep struggling on, and thereby give tacit testimony to a deep conviction that the enterprise of life is worth while.

Let us remember too that when we think of the problem of evil and the arguments against the existence of God which the prevalence of evil raises, there are quite different conclusions that can be drawn from the same evidence. I have mentioned Auschwitz as a symbol of the most depraved evil that has broken out on our planet in recent times. For the first time in history, a sophisticated industrial plant was built especially for the purpose of destroying human beings. For some, like Rabbi Rubenstein, Auschwitz seems like a denial that there is any God directing the history of this world. For others, like Ulrich Simon, Auschwitz demonstrates that the human race is far more deeply in the grip of sin than we have been willing to acknowledge. But it was Dostoyevsky who raised the most disconcerting question of all, in another of his novels, *Crime and Punishment:* 'If there is no God, then is everything permitted?' Or, to express the matter in a different way, 'Do the unprecedented evils that have befallen the human race in the twentieth century demonstrate that there is no God, or has our steadily growing denial of God over the past two hundred years deprived morality of any objective basis, so that now everything is permitted, and, as Nietzsche foresaw, we make and unmake our own values?' Those who advocate the 'permissive society' should ponder these things.

The arguments brought forward by those who advocate a moral or protest atheism raise once more the question of how we conceive God. What kind of God is this who is accused by Camus, Rubenstein, Ivan and others? Is it not once more the monarchical God, the transcendent ruler, the God whose roots are to be found in the pagan empires of antiquity but who ought to have passed into oblivion with the advent of the God of Christianity? For in this new revelation and in its concept of incarnation we think of God working within the world rather than from outside, involved in the happenings of the world rather than untouched by them, sharing even in suffering rather than totally above all pain. When we think of God in this way, then does that not go far to draw the sting of moral atheism?

Admittedly, this more balanced and also more biblical way of thinking about God does not solve the problem of evil, for perhaps there is no solution to that problem available to our minds. But it does neutralize the moral protest against God, which arose from the supposed contrast between a God who lives in the undisturbed bliss of heaven and his suffering creatures here on earth. If God himself is involved more deeply than anyone else in the struggle for the perfecting of the world and the realization of his creation, if God is a self-giving God who is paying in his own substance (his own blood, as it has been symbolized in the language of faith) the price of redemption, then many of the objections to believing in God are removed.

But is it not precisely the God of Christianity who gives of himself in these ways? It was Michael Ramsey, the former Archbishop of Canterbury, who claimed that if theologians, preachers and teachers had been more careful to Christianize their teaching about God, that is to say, to present him as the Christlike God, then probably far fewer people would have drifted away into atheism. For the God of the New Testament and of Christian thought is not just the all-powerful Source of creation and history, as he is imagined still by many people when they hear the name of God. He is the God whose nature is to be interpreted through his manifestation in Jesus Christ, and this revelation, as I said, was nothing less than a revolution in the understanding of God. That revolution culminated in the doctrine of the Trinity, according to which God is not simply the transcendent creator of heaven and earth but is equally the Son who had identified with suffering humanity and has even died on the cross, and is equally the Holy Spirit who groans in travail in bringing to birth the new creation.

Questions and Answers

Q. *The emphasis on the 'indwelling' God is valuable if it takes us away from the popular idea of God as an old man in the sky. But the idea of an indwelling God seems to lack the attribute of 'omnipotence'. Is not omnipotence an essential characteristic of God? Is this position 'ditching' belief in the omnipotence of God?*

A. I am not 'ditching' or trying to get rid of the idea of omnipotence, but I think we have to consider very carefully what 'omnipotence' means. Usually we would think that omnipotence is the capacity to do anything and everything. But when we think about it, we see that even God cannot do anything and everything. St Augustine considered the question in his day. He said there are quite a few things that God cannot do, for instance, God cannot tell a lie. God cannot do this, because it would be contrary to his own nature, as a God of truth. God is not sheer power (as some of the pagan gods perhaps were), his power is always conjoined with and therefore limited by his rationality, his righteousness and, above all, his love. Furthermore, God has created a world to which he has given its own laws and a measure of autonomy. In bringing this created world into being, God has, to some extent, limited his own power. Another theologian of earlier times, St Thomas Aquinas, declared that even God cannot change the past, he cannot go back into history and cause something that has happened not to have happened. To do that would be to violate the very laws that he himself has laid down. If God could change the past, the world would become a nightmare, truly a theatre of the absurd in which we could no longer rely on events following an orderly course. Cosmologists tell us that the world is very finely tuned, so to speak, and if this delicate ordering were even slightly upset, life would speedily become impossible. Stephen Hawkings has remarked 'The laws of science, as we know them at present, contain many fundamental numbers, like the size of the electric charge of the electron and the ratio of the masses of the proton and electron - - - . The remarkable fact is that the values of these numbers seem to have been very finely adjusted to make possible the development of life' (*A Brief History of Time*, Bantam 1988, p. 125). God then cannot do anything that would violate either his own nature or the law-abiding structure that he has given to the world.

Actually in the Bible the words usually translated 'omnipotent' do not imply the power to do anything that one might choose. The Hebrew word *shaddai* in the Old Testament and the Greek word *pantokrator* in the New Testament simply indicate great power, beyond what human beings have. There are many words in English beginning with the syllable 'omni–' but we don't take them in a completely literal sense. We say a dog is omnivorous because it will eat almost any kind of food, but even a dog will not eat everything. Very few would eat a slab of concrete.

Q. *Should we say that God is 'infinite' rather than that he is omnipotent? Creation, by contrast, is finite or limited in its being, whatever is finite must come short of perfection. This finitude or imperfection is the source of evil in the world.*

A. Yes, the Christian faith does think of God as infinite, and it would seem that imperfection must necessarily occur wherever there is finite being. But we must remember that all our language about God is inadequate to describe him – this indeed follows from saying he is infinite. It has been rightly said that 'God retreats in the face of definition' (John Bowker, *The Sense of God*, Oxford University Press 1973, p. 115). We can never have God at our disposal, neatly encapsulated in our language.

Thus even if we say that God is infinite, we have also to say that by creating a universe with its own laws and its own measure of freedom and creativity, God has to that extent limited himself. He has, so to speak, taken a risk in the creation of the world. The free agents in the world (especially we human beings!) may misuse our freedom to frustrate God's purpose in creation. We have in fact done so, but we believe that God in his love has drawn upon his infinite resources to redeem and heal the world. Because God is love as well as power, he has, shall we say, taken the risk of creating a universe, and even put himself at risk in the creation. A vivid symbol of this in provided in the gospels (Mark 6.48) by that picture of Jesus Christ, the incarnate Word, walking on the stormy waters of the lake. God may be infinite, but he has risked himself amid the sufferings and temptations of the finite.

Q. *If it is wrong to think of God chiefly in terms of power and rule, why do we use the Psalms so much in Christian worship?*

A. The Psalms form an incomparable treasury of religious poetry expressing the sense of God's presence, his demands for righteousness and his help. But these ancient poems were written a long time ago and over a long period of years. They are not all of equal value, for the human understanding of God has been much deepened in the course of time. There are indeed some psalms that nowadays we find quite embarrassing, because they express vengeful and vindictive feelings against those who are adjudged to be wicked. One thinks, for example, of Psalms 58 and 109, which one almost never hears sung or recited in church services. No doubt there were times when the Israelites thought of their God in ways very much like those in which the Egyptians or Babylonians thought of Ammon Ra or Marduk.

But on the whole the Psalms lead us towards nobler conceptions of God, and at an early stage in the history of the church, some of these Psalms became inseparably attached to Jesus Christ, and were even supposed to be predictions of his life and death and resurrection and have continued to have a place in the church's liturgies. Examples are Psalm 22, taken to refer to the passion of Jesus Christ, and Psalm 110 which, in spite of its obscurity, has been understood as an affirmation of the messianic and priestly office of Jesus Christ.

3

What about Jesus Christ?

About a year before he was hanged by the Nazis, Dietrich
Bonhoeffer wrote from his prison cell to one of his friends.
In his letter, he said 'The question I keep constantly asking
myself is, "Who really is Jesus Christ for us today?" ' Germany had had a great Christian past, but when Bonhoeffer
was writing, the people in that country had moved not only
into secularism but had embraced a definitely anti-Christian
ideology. Fifty years after Bonhoeffer, we have to ask the
same question, and Christians throughout the entire Western
world have to ask it. The Christianity that was for so many
centuries the spiritual inspiration of the West has, to a large
extent, collapsed. What significance still attaches to Jesus
Christ? Is he no more than a first-century Palestinian peas-
ant? Has he been completely superseded in the advance of
our scientific and technological culture? For many people, he
has become a shadowy figure. They cannot see that he has
anything of importance to contribute to our contemporary
problems. The answers once given to the question, 'Who is
Jesus Christ?' are met either by disbelief or are simply not
understood.

For there was a time when people did think they knew the
answers to the questions about Jesus Christ. They had
learned these answers in the church or the school or the
home. They said that Jesus was the Son of God, or the Christ
or the God-man. They believed that he had died for the sins
of the world, and had risen from the dead, and now offers
eternal salvation to those who place their trust in him. They
believed that he would come again to inaugurate a new age.

They further believed that in the New Testament we have an accurate, even an infallible, account of his deeds and his words. But that whole structure of belief that once seemed so solid and indubitable has been chipped away, bit by bit, and what now remains to us? Biblical criticism, scientific advance, the crumbling of venerable institutions such as the church – these have all placed question marks against the traditional belief in Jesus Christ and force us to ask anew who he is and what is his significance for us.

The very fact that some people are asking anew the questions about Jesus Christ, and asking them with complete seriousness, shows that they are not satisfied just to let Christianity fade out of the picture. That means in turn that they are not satisfied with the 'brave new world' of science and technology. That world is far too ambiguous, and even persons who are not 'religious' in any conventional sense are deeply worried about where contemporary society is going. In spite of the many improvements to the human condition that science and its applications have brought, there is another and less comforting side to the picture – the destructiveness of wars and revolutions, the increase in crime and social unrest, the long-term threats to the environment and even to human survival brought about by the unrestrained exploitation of earth's resources. The material progress of mankind has not been matched by a corresponding moral and spiritual advancement. Greed and aggression are still widespread. So although Christianity has encountered difficulties and has declined quite severely, it has not disappeared. Perhaps only a minority of people, but a considerable minority and an intelligent one, still believes that there is something precious in Christianity and that Jesus Christ still has important meaning for the human race. Perhaps, after all, he *is* God's word to us.

Can Christ really be the God-man, the being in whom divinity and humanity have been united, and can we express that idea in a way that will be understood in the world of today? Is it conceivable that one person can be both God and man, or do we find, when we begin to think about it, that the whole notion of a God-man is nonsensical, a hopelessly mythological figment? I think Christianity can survive only if we can indeed make sense of the God-man. If Christ is to be a Saviour, then he must be truly a human being like ourselves, for if he were some alien type of being, he could have no significance for ourselves in the human condition; whereas, on the other hand, if he does not have something that raises him above the ordinary level of humanity, he cannot open for us the way to a better and fuller life. So we cannot get away from the problem of how this one person, Jesus Christ, somehow unites in himself both the human and the divine.

So let us begin from the human side, and ask whether it is at all possible that a human being might manifest the divine life. This is in fact the path that must have been followed by the very earliest disciples of Jesus. When they first joined themselves to him, they did not immediately attribute to him the full significance that the church was later to give him. They felt themselves attracted, they were impressed by Jesus, but to begin with they thought of him purely as a man, a human being like themselves. Perhaps they thought of him as a prophet or a rabbi, some of them may even have wondered if this was the Christ, but all these ideas remained on the human level. In our oldest gospel, that of Mark (8.29), it was Peter who, in answer to Jesus' own question, 'Who do you say that I am?' replied 'You are the Christ' – though the term 'Christ' was still understood in a purely human way, as designating a man raised up to be a national deliverer.

Perhaps the story of the transfiguration indicates a critical moment in the development of the disciples' understanding of Jesus. He was, we are told, 'transfigured' or 'metamorphosed' before the disciples, so that he appeared to shine with a dazzling light. The disciples heard what they took to be a voice from heaven, attesting Jesus' divine origin: 'This is my beloved Son; listen to him'. One might say that what this story means is that there came a point in the experience of these men when they perceived in Jesus Christ a new depth, a new 'glory' to use the New Testament word, and believed that this was nothing less than the glory of God. With this story, we are already well on the way to the belief that Jesus was not only truly and fully human (something the disciples had never doubted) but that in some sense God was in this man, manifesting his glory in a human life – the event which the church came to call 'incarnation'. But in the experience of the disciples, the starting-point is the humanity of Jesus Christ, and only subsequently does there arise a belief in his divinity.

We have confirmation of this gradual move from thinking of Jesus as simply another human being to the more developed idea that in this human being there came to light a new depth or glory which manifested the glory of God himself, when we look at the way ideas developed in the New Testament itself. The books of the New Testament were written over a period of about sixty years, that is, during the years 40–100 AD. The earliest writings were the letters of Paul. In these letters, Paul is quite unequivocal in recognizing the true humanity of Jesus. So Paul says that Jesus 'was descended from David according to the flesh' (Romans 1.3), that he was 'born of a woman' and, like all other Israelites, 'born under the law' (Galatians 4.4). Again, when Paul expounds his understanding of the person and work of Jesus in two of his major letters (Romans and I Corinthians), it is Christ's humanity which he emphasizes, for he contrasts two human beings, the first Adam who was made in the image of God but fell away from that image into sin, and the new Adam, Jesus Christ, who, through his faithfulness to God, brought the divine image fully to expression, so that Paul can say of him, 'he is the image of the invisible God' (Colossians 1.15), or that we see 'the light of the knowledge of the glory of God in the face of Christ' (II Corinthians 4.6). The same teaching that we find in Paul, teaching that begins from Jesus in his humanity and goes on to claim that in this very humanity there comes to light the glory of

God, is found somewhat differently expressed in other early parts of the New Testament. A good example is found in the early sermons preserved in the opening chapters of Acts. On the Feast of Pentecost, Peter preached to the people, saying, 'Let all the house of Israel know assuredly that God has made him both Lord and Christ, this Jesus whom you crucified.'

But when we come to the latest writings of the New Testament we find that the old story about Jesus has been turned around, so that it begins no longer from his humanity but from his divinity. The classic example is the beginning of John's gospel. It is the story not of a human being who is raised to God or who is transfigured so as to manifest God, but the story of a divine being, the eternal Word or Logos, who was in the beginning with God in the heavenly realm and then comes down to mankind. This story begins from above, so to speak: 'In the beginning was the Word, and the Word was with God, and the Word was God – and the Word was made flesh and dwelt among us, full of grace and truth.' This new version of the story may well be more profound than the first one. We should expect it to be more profound, for John's gospel comes near the end of those sixty years or so in which the New Testament was written, so there had been quite a long time to reflect on the fuller meaning of Jesus Christ since the days when Paul was writing his letters or Peter was preaching his sermons. But it is important to understand that the second story does not abolish the first one and should not allow us to forget the first one. It is the first story that forces us to take seriously the humanity of Christ, and without that true humanity he could not relate to us in any meaningful way.

After the last books of the New Testament had been written, the church went on thinking about Jesus Christ, how he relates to us and how he relates to God. More than three hundred years had passed before what we call the Nicene Creed was promulgated in a form very like that which it still has. When we look at this creed, we see that it has followed the second story, the one found in John's gospel, and that the earlier story, which stressed Jesus' human experience, is not given much prominence. We speak in the most exalted terms of Christ's divinity, saying that he is 'the only Son of God, eternally begotten of the Father, God from God, Light from Light, true God from true God, begotten, not made, of one being with the Father.' Only then do we go on to affirm that 'he came down from heaven; by the power of the Holy Spirit he became incarnate of the Virgin Mary and was made man.' So in this creed, his humanity is put firmly in second place, and the overwhelming stress is on his deity.

That way of understanding Christ has persisted for centuries, and the earlier way of thinking has been, if not forgotten, at least, pushed very much into the background. The result has been, almost inevitably, to dim down the true humanity of our Lord and to encourage the tendency against which Bishop Robinson and many others protested, of thinking of Christ in terms so exclusively divine that he becomes a somewhat unreal figure, a visitor from beyond rather than a person who truly belongs to this world. And if Jesus is not truly and fully a man, then surely that nullifies any claim that he is the God-man or that there has been anything that may be regarded as a genuine incarnation of God.

These remarks on how the human Jesus became the bearer and revealer of the divine life bring us back to the more general question – how is it possible for any human being to be the revelation or manifestation of God? At this point we must notice an important claim that is made about the human being all through the Bible, and that is especially applied to Jesus Christ. The claim goes back to the creation stories at the beginning of Genesis. After he had created the material world and then the plants and then the animals, God said: 'Let us make man in our own image and likeness.' The writer goes on to say that God did in fact make the first man and the first woman in his image and likeness, and this clearly means that in some degree all human beings had a share in God's own mode of being. In some way, on the level of the finite, they had a share in the wisdom, power and creativity of God. In other words, there is some deep affinity or analogy between God and the human creature. The point is reaffirmed in the second chapter of Genesis where God is said to have breathed his own living breath into the man that he had formed from the dust of the earth.

Now, in the days when Genesis was written, the Hebrews probably had no conception of such ideas as evolution and development. But in the second century after Christ, some Greek theologians were beginning to interpret the old creation stories in terms of the evolution or transcendence of human beings to higher stages of existence. Irenaeus, bishop of Lyons, saw that human beings cannot be produced ready-made, so to speak, like manufactured objects coming off a production line. They need time and history to develop, they need experience and perhaps even suffering. Thus, to say that they were made in the image of God could only mean that they had the potentiality of developing toward God. Their final destiny would be likeness to God, when they would fully manifest the image or icon of God on the finite level. So Irenaeus held that Adam and Eve must have begun as children, not adults. They had to grow and this needed time.

There is of course some support for this view in the Bible itself. We have noted that Paul drew a comparison between the first Adam and Jesus Christ, whom he regarded as the new or second Adam. The first Adam had the potentiality of growing toward God, but he failed to develop in this way, falling into sin, and that has been the common lot of the human race. But the new Adam, Jesus Christ, remained faithful even to the cross, so that he is, in Paul's words, the image of the invisible God. The early Christian theologians did not hesitate to speak of a deification of man, a process of growing into the likeness of God. It is in some such way as this that we can begin to envisage how it is possible for a human being to become the bearer and manifestation of the divine life, or how there is the possibility of a divine humanity.

It is interesting to observe that modern philosophical ideas of the human being show a remarkable convergence with those traditional biblical and theological teachings. An insight that runs through virtually all modern studies of humanity, both philosophical and scientific (for instance, Rahner, *Spirit in the World* (Sheed & Ward 1968) and Bloch, *Principle of Hope* (Blackwell 1986)), is that humanity is unfinished, it is still on its way, developing toward a goal which is not yet fully disclosed. These words remind us of a verse in the New Testament: 'See what love the Father has given us, that we should be called children of God; and so we are – Beloved, we are God's children now; it does not yet appear what we shall be, but we know that when he appears, we shall be like him' (I John 3.2).

Now this insight has been largely accepted in modern secular theories of the human person, except that these secular theories will usually leave out the mention of God. But remarkable similarities remain. There is no such thing as a fixed human nature, unchanging for all time. Humanity is in process of forming its nature. The secular expression of this insight derives in part from the evolutionary theories of the nineteenth century, but also from some philosophical theories of the past one hundred and fifty years or so. Among these philosophical sources is existentialism, the view which thinks of a human being as a creative centre, welling up in the world, and then faced with the task of working at becoming that being which he or she has chosen as the ideal. One of the early existentialists, Friedrich Neitzsche, compared the human species to a bridge, an intermediate stage between an animal past and a future which he called the 'superman', a higher level of existence which is the secular equivalent of the God-man of theology. Other types of philosophy have taught similar doctrines. When we begin to think in such ways, we see what is meant by the idea of a human being rising toward God and entering into a union with God, the idea of the God-man. Such an idea is certainly not nonsensical. This is how the Christian may interpret Jesus Christ. In him, the divine reality has shone forth – in the words of

John's gospel (1.14), 'We have beheld his glory, glory as of the only begotten of the Father.'

But that is only one side of the story. A human being, even Jesus Christ, could rise to God only if God had already deeply descended into him. God himself is the author and originator of incarnation. Although Paul thought of Jesus Christ as the new Adam, he also declares, 'All this is from God' (II Corinthians 5.18).

People have difficulty in believing in incarnation, that God was in Christ, because they often start out with some preconceived idea of God that makes incarnation virtually impossible. If one thinks of God as a static unchanging being at an infinite distance from the world, then incarnation seems impossible. But the God of Christian faith is not like that. He is a living God. Just as the creatures are constantly transcending themselves, so God too surpasses himself, going forth in creative power into the creation.

That is what we mean by saying that from the beginning the Word was with God and the Word was God. A word is that which comes forth from someone and reveals what has hitherto been hidden in that person's mind. At the same time, the word is so close to the person who utters it that it may be regarded as a part or extension of the speaker. This is what we mean when we say in the creed that Jesus Christ is 'one in being' or 'of one substance' with the Father.

God speaks his word, and in a sense he expresses himself in the whole creation. But clearly he is more fully expressed in some parts of it than in others. He is more fully expressed in a person than, let us say, in a hydrogen atom, for a person, as we have seen, has some share in the power and wisdom of God and can even grow into likeness to God. So if God wills to express himself in the creation, we must look at the being who would be most truly able to be the vehicle for that expression, namely, a human being who exhibits the image of God in its fullness, and this, I have tried to show you, is Jesus Christ.

So what about Jesus Christ? We can do no better than

repeat the words of Paul: 'He is the image' – or the icon –
'of the invisible God.'

Questions and Answers

Q. *Do we have a unique revelation in Jesus Christ?*

A. There is of course a sense in which Jesus Christ is
indeed a unique figure. There is no one quite like him, and
for those of us who are Christians, he is the source and centre
of what we know about God. But this uniqueness does not
mean that only in Jesus Christ and nowhere else can God be
known. There is a sense in which God is present in the whole
of his creation and can be known to some extent through
his creation. So a Christian will not deny that there is a
knowledge of God in the non-Christian religions or even in
what is sometimes called 'natural' religion, that is to say, the
sense of God or of the holy, however vague it may be, that
many people have in the face of the grandeur and beauty of
the creation. St Thomas Aquinas tells us 'God is in everything, by substance, power and presence.' But he is not equally present in everything or equally revealed in everything.
As I have tried to show, the fullest revelation of God could
come only in and through that creature who is made in the
image of God, and such, we claim, is Jesus Christ.

Q. *If there are truths about God in non-Christian religions,
would this suggest a merging or unification of religions, as
in the Baha'i movement?*

A. As we learn about the different religions of the world,
we do see that they have many beliefs in common, and it
seems right that they should work together in some matters,
for instance, in the promotion of world peace. But the
attempt to merge them into some composite faith is, I think,

mistaken. Although Baha'i, to take the example cited, began only in the nineteenth century, there have always been a few people who have advocated and sometimes practised what is called 'syncretism', a form of religion which combines the teachings of many faiths. At the beginning of the third century, there was a Roman emperor, Alexander Severus, who had a chapel containing busts of Apollo, Moses, Jesus and other great religious leaders. But the trouble about such multi-faith religions is that they overlook the differences between the traditions which they try to incorporate, and often end up with something merely superficial and sentimental.

Any faith, whether it is Christianity or Islam or Buddhism or something else, has to be studied in depth if we are taking it seriously, and we cannot do that if we are trying to spread ourselves over half a dozen faiths at once. Furthermore, if we really get into one faith and understand it, I think that this is the best way to develop a sympathetic understanding of other faiths.

Q. *Does the idea of the transcendence of the human being and the advance from the first Adam to the new Adam imply human progress, or may there also be degeneration?*

A. Christianity has always rejected the idea that there is any automatic progress of the human race. Certainly the idea has been common in Europe for several centuries, and seemed to be confirmed by the theory of evolution. But although human beings have progressed in knowledge and in the mastery of their environment, there does not seem to have been any corresponding progress in moral and in spiritual sensitivity. If human beings have the possibility of transcending themselves, the price of this seems to be that they can also slip back. But although Christian faith does not accept the idea of a constant human progress, it takes a hopeful view because it believes that men and women have been created in the divine image. This is like a conscience within ourselves, directing us into those ways that lead to a fuller humanity, and directing us away from those ways that diminish our humanity. Jesus Christ, as the human being who has signally fulfilled human life in the image and likeness of God, is not the sign of a universal human progress but he does show us and helps us to attain this goal.

Q. *Is the difference between Jesus Christ and other human beings one of degree, or is it a difference of kind?*

A. This is a controversial question and all Christians would not give the same answer. My own view, however, would be that the difference is one of degree. I say this because it is important for us to think of Jesus Christ as fully sharing our humanity. If that is denied, then it is difficult or impossible to see how he could be relevant to us or how we could acknowledge him as Saviour. This point is made very strongly in the New Testament, especially in the Epistle to the Hebrews. Jesus is depicted there as the great High Priest between God and man, and it is declared that he can fulfil this office only if he has really known the human condition and shared in its sufferings and temptations.

Q. *If God is in everything, is there any difference between Christianity and pantheism?*

A. Pantheism is a somewhat vague belief, and there are several varieties of it. Usually the pantheist thinks of God as wholly immanent in the world, so that in fact God comes to be virtually identified with the world. Christianity does acknowledge God's immanence in the world, but does not believe that he is wholly immanent. God is both within the world and over the world.

This is expressed in the doctrine of the Trinity. God the Father is over the world which he has created, God the Son has lived in the world and in human history, God the Holy

Spirit indwells the world and strives to bring creation to its perfection.

Q. *Why did the incarnation happen at the time it did?*

A. The first answer to that question is, 'I do not know – perhaps only God knows'. A second answer is that I can only hazard a guess, following some of the guesses made by early Fathers of the church. The guess is that Jesus was born at a time when several currents of events all seemed to converge upon him.

The first current was the history of Israel, with its expectations of a messiah, and the further expectation, strong at that time, that the old age had run its course and that God was about to bring in a new age. The message of both Jesus and John the Baptist was, 'The kingdom of heaven is at hand!'

The second current was Greek philosophy. As early as the year 150, Justin the Martyr was claiming that such Greek thinkers as Socrates and Heraclitus had lived 'according to the Word' before the Word was made flesh in Jesus. In the reign of Augustus, the first Roman emperor, poets including Virgil were announcing that a new age was about to begin.

Finally, it seemed to some minds that the Roman empire, which had established a relative peace all through the Mediterranean world and had built up a road system that made communication easy over the whole area, was a kind of providential preparation for the spread of a universal gospel. So the early church historian, Eusebius, did not hesitate to speak of a *Preparatio evangelica*, a preparation for the gospel, and saw in these events the 'fullness of time', of which Paul had spoken as marking the time of the coming of Jesus.

4

Do We Need the Church?

After we have been thinking of such exalted themes as God and Jesus Christ, it may seem something of an anticlimax when we are asked to turn our minds to the church. Compared with the divine realities, the church seems all too human, flawed and earthly. We sometimes hear people declaring that while they acknowledge the virtues of Christianity, they want nothing to do with Churchianity, as they call it. A historian and biblical scholar, Alfred Loisy, once remarked that Jesus Christ promised us the kingdom of God, but instead, we got the church. That was meant to be a pretty devastating remark, and it does in fact remind us that the church is a very imperfect instrument for fulfilling whatever purposes God has for it. So I think we must begin by resolving not to be carried away by ideas of the church that are too idealized or that exaggerate what is good about the church and turn a blind eye to the many things that are wrong with it. We use certain high-sounding phrases to describe the church, and while they may indeed tell us what the church ought to be, they may be far from the truth of what the church actually is. We say, for instance, that the church is 'the extension of the incarnation' or that it is the 'body of Christ' or the 'people of God', and these expressions all tell us what the church might be and even should be, but in fact it falls so short of these ideals that we come close to trivializing these expressions when we apply them to the actual church.

The church, whatever it ought to be or whatever it may eventually become, is decidedly not yet the kingdom of God or the people of God in any convincing sense. So I think we can understand why many people who may believe in God and who may have been deeply impressed by Jesus Christ feel that they cannot respond in the same affirmative way to the church. Some of them would go so far as to argue that the church has turned away from the teachings and concerns of Jesus and has lost itself in the pursuit of various worldly ambitions. Even if the church was pure in the beginning, it soon lost its way in amassing wealth and acquiring lands and property, or in seeking political power. Today every church in Christendom has developed a complex bureaucracy, so that it is hard to see any essential difference between the churches and all the other bureaucratic institutions that proliferate in the contemporary world.

But in spite of the various faults which at any time disfigure the church, we also see from time to time what may be called 'gleams of glory', moments when the ideal nature of the church, its true nature, shines out. This happens, for instance, in the lives of the saints, men and women who, through their self-sacrifice and the help that they give to others, show us the genuine spirit of Christianity and in their own way follow in the steps of Jesus Christ so that in them we may indeed speak of a continuation of the incarnation and of the Body of Christ existing in the world. And sometimes this is true not only of exceptional individuals but of the church or some part of it as a community, standing up to persecution in a hostile environment or bringing a new wave of faith and hope in a time of despondency and anxiety.

Ideally, every Christian should be worthy of the name of 'saint', as seems to have been assumed in New Testament times, and every period in the life of the Christian community should maintain a high level of faith and obedience. But this is not an ideal world, and the church, like everything else in the world, has its ups and downs. In the days after Pentecost, its life burned brightly, and it seemed indeed to be advancing toward the goal of the kingdom of God. But the flame died down, and since then it has burned only fitfully. Sometimes it has nearly gone out, then it has blazed up again and we have been shown that the church is not dead, that the vivifying Spirit of God still lives in the church, and that perhaps after all we can believe the gospel (Matthew 16.18) that 'the gates of hell will not prevail against it'.

In the statement of the Christian faith which we call the Nicene Creed we say 'We believe in one holy catholic and apostolic church'. These four adjectives – *one, holy, catholic, apostolic*, are known as the 'notes' of the church, its distinguishing marks. Obviously, when these words were chosen to set out the distinctive nature of the church, those who chose them were thinking of the church in its ideal condition, rather than the church that Christians know in their actual parishes and congregations. But we must keep that ideal vision of the church before us as something to strive after, a stage on the way to the kingdom of God in its fullness. It will therefore be helpful to us to consider these four marks of the church one after the other, both to ask ourselves how far we are falling short of them at the present time and to take up the challenge of realizing them more adequately. Since the church itself has two sides to it, both an inward spiritual side described by the four notes, and the outward, visible side that we see in the world around us, we shall find that each of the four has embodiment in some visible form that has its place in the historical church.

Let us begin then with the first of the four notes. We believe that the church is *one*. The church bears or should bear the mark of unity, in accordance with our Lord's own prayer in the great discourses of John's gospel (17.11), when he said: 'Holy father, keep them in thy name, which thou hast given me, that they may be one, even as we are one.' This unity that Christ asked for his church is one that exceeds anything that we can imagine, for it is compared by him with the perfect unity that binds together the Father and the Son within the triune being of God. It is a unity beyond anything we know on earth or anything in even the highest reaches of human experience.

It contrasts sharply with the nature of the visible church as we know it. So often the church is rent by quarrels, many of them of a somewhat petty nature, though sometimes, especially in the sixteenth and seventeenth centuries, they took the form of religious wars that were fought with a savagery which still disgraces the history of the church. How can we possibly claim that the church is one in the face of such clear proofs to the contrary?

Perhaps, in spite of all, there has lingered in the church a deep sense of its underlying unity, springing from the Lord's own prayer for his church. Perhaps it was that sense that awakened in the church what we call the ecumenical movement, the deliberate striving to overcome hostile divisions and to achieve a visible unity in the church as it is perceived by the world. Unfortunately, that striving after visible unity has itself been badly affected by the bureaucratic tendencies of the present age, and endless time has been spent in trying to merge the various churches and denominations on an organizational basis. The unity of which Jesus spoke was something far more fundamental – a unity of love analogous to that supreme love which unites the Father and the Son. Such a love would do far more than any merger of separate Christian churches, for it would provide a model for a new unity among the many races and nations of human beings, many of whom are still divided by deep hostilities and even, in some parts of the world, engaged in physical conflict with each other. Indeed, the different denominations with their varying liturgies and polities may even be helping the Christian cause by showing that it is possible to maintain a healthy diversity of forms of Christianity, thus widening its appeal to the diversity of human beings, as can be seen in the United States.

But too much diversity leads in the long run to dissolution, unless there is some unifying framework. This would be the visible embodiment corresponding to the inward spiritual unity of the church. This outward embodiment is simply the Bible. All Christian bodies which claim to be churches have a common allegiance to the Bible. They all agree in recognizing the books of the Old and New Testaments as having a supreme authority in defining what Christianity is. That is already a very large measure of unity from which to begin, and can lead eventually to a more extensive and visible unity of the church than we currently have. Then we shall be able to say with a better conscience. 'We believe in *one* holy catholic and apostolic church', and will be able more honestly to commend the Christian faith as a way to unity in the wider world.

We claim also that the church is *holy*. Again we are looking here to the ideal, rather than to the actual state of affairs. We do find holiness in the church and we know that holiness belongs to its true nature. But there is much in its life that is unholy. It has often seemed to me, for instance, that ecclesiastical politics are even more disreputable than those of Parliament. But this should not be, for the work of the church is sanctification, that is to say, making holy. First, making its own members holy, then sanctifying the whole creation, both human and non-human. Again there is good biblical precedent for this: 'As he who called you is holy, be holy yourselves in all your conduct; since it is written, "you shall be holy, for I am holy"' (I Peter 1.15). What an impossible demand! That we human beings should measure ourselves against the holiness of God and his Christ?

But there is a means whereby even sinful human beings can be set at least part of the way towards holiness, and those whom we call saints have shown that it is possible to progress quite a long way. For corresponding to the holiness of the church we find once again a visible, embodied means by which God's grace descends into human hearts and allows men and women to ascend towards him. I refer, of course, to the *sacraments* of the church, those visible and outward signs of an inward and invisible grace. The word 'sacrament' has been used chiefly of baptism and the eucharist, both explicitly enjoined in the New Testament, but sometimes it is used in a very wide sense; Christ, the church and even the world having been called sacraments because they can all be understood as visible manifestations which put us in touch with God. Usually, however, we think of seven sacraments which span human life from its beginning to its end, making the divine grace accessible at every stage, and so making possible a life that can be truly sanctified.

1. The first sacrament is *baptism*. It brings us into the church and incorporates the life of the baptized person into the life of Jesus Christ. As Paul describes it, it is a dying with Christ and a rising with him to new life. It is like a second birth. Our first natural birth is into a world marred by sin, while baptism brings a new beginning, a life in the Spirit of Christ mediated to us through the community of the Spirit.

2. Next, there is *confirmation*. In the early days of the church, this sacrament was joined with baptism in a single rite of initiation. After the baptism with water, the baptized person was signed with the sign of the cross using oil, a part of the rite that was called consignation. Later this was separated from the water baptism, and became the sacrament of confirmation. It simply re-emphasizes what happens in baptism, especially the gift of the Holy Spirit so that the person confirmed is equipped for the trials of life and drawn toward sanctification.

3. Thirdly, we note the sacrament of *penance* or *reconciliation*. Again if we go back to the early church, we get a clue to the meaning. It was at one time believed that after having been baptized, no one should sin again, and it was even believed that sin committed after baptism could not be forgiven. But it was soon found that this was too hard a demand to make on sinful human beings. Also, our Lord had taught that we should be willing to forgive seventy times seven. Could God be less forgiving than men were asked to be? At first, the leaders of the church said 'Well, you can have one sin forgiven after baptism, but no more!' Of course, that rule also was too harsh. Gradually the church moved on to the present practice. When sin comes between us and God and

our conscience cannot be quieted, the Prayer Book urges us to make confession to a priest as Christ's representative, and to hear through him the word of absolution. Again, this is an important help toward a more sanctified life.

4. In the middle of this list of seven, I place the *eucharist* as the greatest of all the sacraments. I said that the church has sometimes been called the extension of the incarnation. This is above all true of the church when it celebrates the eucharist. Christ, we believe, is really present with us in this rite which he instituted for the remembrance of him, and we also plead before the Father Christ's eternal sacrifice on our behalf. Our receiving of the consecrated bread and wine is a receiving in our hearts of his very life, so that, in the words of the Prayer Book, 'we may evermore dwell in him and he in us'. This surely carries sanctification as far as it can go in this life.

5. *Marriage* too is brought into the sacramental category. In the union of man and woman in marriage and in the family which normally follows from it, the most intimate and formative human relationships are developed. Especially in our own time, we have witnessed the tragedy of the down-grading of these relationships and the consequent impoverishment of human life. The restoration of a truly sacramental understanding of marriage would be a major step toward building a new respect and reverence for one another and so toward building a more human and more Christian community.

6. Some, though not all, Christians receive the gift of *ordination*. All Christians have a ministry to their brothers and sisters, a ministry which they receive in baptism and confirmation. But some are set aside for a special ministry, and it is they who have the heavy responsibility of preaching the word of God and dispensing the sacraments. They are not to be thought of as somehow holier than the lay people of God. Christ himself is the true minister of every sacrament, therefore the validity of the sacrament does not depend at all on the virtues of the minister but simply on his being

authorized to represent Christ in that sacrament. So St Augustine could say – and perhaps it shocked his hearers – whether you are baptized by St Peter or by Judas Iscariot makes no difference, because the real minister is always Jesus Christ.

7. Finally there is the sacrament of *unction*, a very ancient rite that goes back to New Testament times and is mentioned in the Epistle of James (5.14). For a long time, this sacrament was called 'extreme' unction, because it was given only at the end of life to strengthen the person in the face of death. It is now offered in any serious illness. It is not, of course, an alternative to medicine, but it can bring calm and encouragement to those facing the rigours of sickness.

There is so much to be said about the sacraments that they would deserve another book in themselves, but enough has been said to show that the description of the church as holy is not an empty boast, for in these holy rites she has been entrusted with means of grace. Though some things in the church's record may make us uneasy or even ashamed, the fact that she is the guardian and dispenser of the sacraments should remind us of the incalculable debt that men and women have owed to the church as the channel through which God's grace has reached them.

The church is one, holy and also *catholic*. This third note of the church speaks chiefly of its universality. It is for all mankind and stretches through both time and space. 'Catholic' means much more than just the opposite of 'Protestant'. The Catholic branches of the church (Orthodox, Roman Catholic, Anglican) stress the continuity of the present-day church with the original Christian community founded by Jesus Christ. There is a famous definition of 'catholicity' by St Vincent of Lerins soon after the year 400: that which has been accepted in all places, at all times, by all Christians. In other words, there is a Christian identity that remains constant. This does not rule out all possibility of change and development, but it does set bounds to it. There are changes so radical that they would not be developments within Christianity but rather the establishment of a new religion. This is the kind of test that has to be applied to new sects and denominations.

Again, there is an outward embodiment of this note of the church, and that is the catholic creeds. From the beginning, there was a rule of faith, a brief summary of the essentials of Christianity. In course of time, this was formulated in the form of creeds. Perhaps the best known is the Apostles' Creed, though the most ecumenical and widely used is the Nicene Creed. The Prayer Book added to these the Athanasian Creed, but it is a much more technical statement. But we recite these creeds as the visible token of our adherence to the one catholic church of the ages.

There is one further note to discuss – the church is *apostolic*. In some ways, this is not very different from saying it is catholic. It is the claim to be the same church as that of the apostles and therefore to have maintained the authentic Christian faith through all the vicissitudes of history. This is the doctrine of apostolic succession, the belief that the church of today believes and teaches and enacts, though in changed circumstances, all that the apostles embraced in the earliest and purest days of the church.

Here again there is a clear visible embodiment of that vital link with the apostles, namely, the apostolic ministry, in its classical threefold form of bishops, priests and deacons. The continuity of the church from its origins has not been simply the passing on of scriptures, dogmas, rites and ceremonies, but a personal continuity in which bishop has succeeded bishop in a community which, when it has been true to itself, has been formed by reverence, faithfulness, love, and, not least, by outreach to those beyond its borders.

Do we need the church? It is hard for us sometimes not to become impatient with its blundering ways, but that can be put right only if we are all resolved to do better for the church. If we tried to live as individual Christians, we would be even weaker and more ineffective than the church. We need the support of the church's community, its worship, its scriptures, its sacraments. It is the living instrument that God himself has appointed for the communication of his grace. We are thankful for what it has brought us, and since we ourselves are the church, let us live up to what it demands of us.

Questions and Answers

Q. *Is there room for post-Christian revelation? There have obviously been changes in Christian belief and practice, for instance, the abolition of slavery in the nineteenth century. Were the reasons for these changes already present in germ in the original faith?*

A. This question raises important and controversial issues. I do not myself like the expression, 'post-Christian revelation'. It is true that in some charismatic and mystical sects, individuals have occasionally claimed to have experienced an 'inner light,' which to them was so intense that it had more authority than the tradition of the church or even than the scriptures. But such experiences are so individualistic that the mainstream Christian churches and denominations have usually regarded them as errors or deviations from the catholic or authentic Christian faith. To deserve the name of Christian, that faith must be seen as continuous with the teaching of the apostles. So in the early centuries the church agreed on the 'canon' of the New Testament, that is to say, they agreed on the list of books to be included in the New Testament as having authority; and in the same period there was devised the 'rule of faith', a brief statement of the church's faith, which at first varied slightly from place to place but was eventually formulated in the catholic creeds, as I have described. Now this does not mean that Christianity was fixed (or, if you like, fossilized) in the language and formulae of the early centuries, but it does mean that when some apparently new doctrine or practice is proposed, it has to be measured against the canonical scriptures and the catholic creeds.

I have mentioned that St Vincent of Lerins proposed a test which came to be widely accepted. He offered as a guideline that 'what has been believed in all places, at all times, and by all Christians' is to be regarded as the true catholic faith. But a few paragraphs later in his book, Vincent wrote that there should be a great development of understanding of the faith as the centuries roll on, so he was not trying to arrest the understanding of the faith at one particular point. The creeds had still some fluidity in his day, and, in any case, the meanings of words change and he was not ruling out new formulations or even new interpretations. But there had to be at the same time some continuity. Something entirely innovative or something contradicting clear New Testament or credal teaching could not be regarded as truly catholic.

The whole problem of doctrinal development in the church was raised anew in the nineteenth century, especially in a famous book by John Henry Newman, *An Essay in the Development of Doctrine*. The first edition was published in 1845 while Newman was still vicar of the University church: the definitive edition came in 1878 after he had moved to Roman Catholicism. Newman's main purpose was to show that certain doctrines taught in modern times by the Roman Catholic Church have their germ (to use the word chosen in the question) in the earliest Christianity, though they are not explicit there. But he also provided some very useful tests for ascertaining what developments in the general teaching of the churches may be regarded as legitimate.

Let me give two examples of current developments that need to be tested. One is the change in the practice (if not the doctrine) of priesthood brought about through the ordination of women. This is not something that could be argued from scripture alone, but it might be claimed to be a legitimate development. It would, however, have difficulties in maintaining itself in the face of Vincent's third test, general consent. A second example is the so-called 'death of God' theology discussed in the chapter 'Believing in God', and in the more recent 'non-realist theology' of Don Cupitt and others, according to whom God has no real or objective existence as creator, judge, redeemer, or any of the other things that have been traditionally assigned to him, but is himself a creature of the human mind. As far as I can see, this has no roots in traditional Christianity and has to be rejected as a sub-Christian aberration.

Q. *Didn't the attempt to devise tests of catholicity arise from a desire to exclude those from whom the devisers of the test differed?*

A. Unfortunately there is a tendency among all religious people, both Christians and non-Christians, to enforce their beliefs on others and to condemn those who believe otherwise. For the proof of this, one has only to think of the long and disgraceful history of persecutions and wars carried out in the name of religion. Yet no religion can survive without some definition of its beliefs and practices. If everything is permissible, then that religion has ceased to stand for anything. It is very likely that there is so much 'fundamentalism' and intolerance around today because the churches have become so vague about their beliefs and so wishy-washy in their ethics.

It is very hard to proclaim a faith that has enough substance and definite shape that it can meet people's spiritual needs, and yet at the same time is flexible enough to accommodate those who have honest doubts and questions.

Our faith, if it is to have meaning and effect in our lives, has to be a *committed* faith: but at the same time it must be *open* to the insights that come from other faiths and to the doubts and questions of seekers after truth, inside or outside the church.

Further Reading

The four chapters of this book provide only the most elementary introduction to Christianity. Those who find it an interesting subject will want to go on reading and learning more – and the subject is so vast that one could spend a whole lifetime in further reading!

British readers seem to prefer short books, while our continental friends are more willing to take on lengthy volumes. But if you would like to tackle a long (but not difficult) book that will give you a panoramic view of Christian faith, I would recommend *On Being a Christian*, by Hans Küng (1977, SCM Press 1991), perhaps the most widely read theologian of our time.

There are many books about God, and one of the best to appear for a long time is *The Christlike God*, by John V. Taylor, formerly Bishop of Winchester and now resident in Oxford (SCM Press 1992). It is also worth while going back to look at the late John Robinson's *Honest to God* (SCM Press 1963), which caused such a stir thirty years ago, and if you read that book, follow it up with the same author's *Exploration into God* (from the library or second-hand), a less controversial but more thoughtful book.

On Jesus Christ, one ought to begin with the New Testament, the main or, indeed, the only source of our knowledge about him. But the New Testament has to be read with the help of modern scholarship. Get hold of Dennis Nineham's *Gospel of Mark* (Penguin Books 1969). This book contains the text of the gospel with illuminating comments by Professor Nineham.

There are innumerable books on Jesus, some dealing with the history, others with his significance for faith. *Jesus the Jew* by Geza Vermes (1973, SCM Press 1983) is a strictly historical study, showing us how Jesus might have appeared to his own people in his own time. Another historical study is *Jesus and Judaism* by Edward P. Sanders (SCM Press 1980), longer than the Vermes book and widely acclaimed. John Macquarrie's *Jesus Christ in Modern Thought* (SCM Press 1990) is concerned with the ways in which Christians have thought of Jesus and with the question of faith in Jesus in our own time.

On the church, it is a good idea to go back to read about the origins and what the church was seeking to become in its early days. Henry Chadwick's *The Early Church* (Penguin Books 1967) is an obvious choice. As for the church struggling in the modern secularized world, a very fair study can be found in Alister McGrath's *The Renewal of Anglicanism* (SPCK 1993).

Quite a few questions are raised about the relation of Christianity to other faiths. This is a subject that has attracted much attention in recent years and again there are many books about it. A good introduction is *Christian Theology and Inter-religious Dialogue*, by Maurice Wiles (SCM Press 1992).

All books nowadays are expensive, and some very expensive. But I think nearly all of those mentioned are in print as paperbacks, and in any case you should be able to get the books through your local library. Happy reading!

Index